Set design by Robert Morgan *Photo by Terry Shapiro*

Kathleen M. Brady as Bernice in the Denver Center Theatre Company production of *Bernice/Butterfly*.

BERNICE/ BUTTERFLY

A TWO-PART INVENTION

BY NAGLE JACKSON

DRAMATISTS
PLAY SERVICE
INC.

BERNICE/BUTTERFLY
Copyright © 2007, Nagle Jackson

All Rights Reserved

CAUTION: Professionals and amateurs are hereby warned that performance of BERNICE/BUTTERFLY is subject to payment of a royalty. It is fully protected under the copyright laws of the United States of America, and of all countries covered by the International Copyright Union (including the Dominion of Canada and the rest of the British Commonwealth), and of all countries covered by the Pan-American Copyright Convention, the Universal Copyright Convention, the Berne Convention, and of all countries with which the United States has reciprocal copyright relations. All rights, including without limitation professional/amateur stage rights, motion picture, recitation, lecturing, public reading, radio broadcasting, television, video or sound recording, all other forms of mechanical, electronic and digital reproduction, transmission and distribution, such as CD, DVD, the Internet, private and file-sharing networks, information storage and retrieval systems, photocopying, and the rights of translation into foreign languages are strictly reserved. Particular emphasis is placed upon the matter of readings, permission for which must be secured from the Author's agent in writing.

The English language stock and amateur stage performance rights in the United States, its territories, possessions and Canada for BERNICE/BUTTERFLY are controlled exclusively by DRAMATISTS PLAY SERVICE, INC., 440 Park Avenue South, New York, NY 10016. No professional or nonprofessional performance of the Play may be given without obtaining in advance the written permission of DRAMATISTS PLAY SERVICE, INC., and paying the requisite fee.

Inquiries concerning all other rights should be addressed to Harden-Curtis Associates, 850 Seventh Avenue, Suite 903, New York, NY 10019. Attn: Mary Harden.

SPECIAL NOTE
Anyone receiving permission to produce BERNICE/BUTTERFLY is required to give credit to the Author as sole and exclusive Author of the Play on the title page of all programs distributed in connection with performances of the Play and in all instances in which the title of the Play appears for purposes of advertising, publicizing or otherwise exploiting the Play and/or a production thereof. The name of the Author must appear on a separate line, in which no other name appears, immediately beneath the title and in size of type equal to 50% of the size of the largest, most prominent letter used for the title of the Play. No person, firm or entity may receive credit larger or more prominent than that accorded the Author. The following acknowledgment must appear on the title page in all programs distributed in connection with performances of the Play:

BERNICE/BUTTERFLY received its world premiere
at the Denver Center Theatre Company,
Donovan Marley, Artistic Director, January 2, 2002.

For
Kathleen Brady
and
Jamie Horton

BERNICE/BUTTERFLY received its world premiere at Denver Center Theatre Company (Donovan Marley, Artistic Director; Barbara E. Sellers, Producing Director) on January 2, 2002. It was directed by Nagle Jackson; the set design was by Robert Morgan; the costume design was by Kevin Copenhaver; the lighting design was by Dawn Chiang; the sound design was by David R. White; the stage manager was Lyle Raper; and the assistant stage manager was Victoria Ravenscroft. The cast was as follows:

BERNICE .... Kathleen M. Brady
RANDALL .... Jamie Horton
TOMMY .... Mark Rubald

CHARACTERS

BERNICE
RANDALL
TOMMY

PLACE

PART ONE: BERNICE AT BAY
The O-Kay Diner in central Kansas.

PART TWO: THE BUTTERFLY EFFECT
A speaker's platform.

TIME

The present.

BERNICE/BUTTERFLY

PART ONE

BERNICE AT BAY

A small diner. The counter, with seven stools. To the right, a small cashier's counter with a simple, old-fashioned adding machine and a spindle where paid checks are stacked. The spindle is empty. To the left, a partitioned off-space which we cannot see, behind which the coffee machines and a refrigerator are apparently kept. Upstage, center, is a pass-thru to the kitchen.

All the accoutrements of a diner: a pastry case, a milkshake blender, etc., but everything is empty. No actual food is ever seen. There is a stack of plates and bowls on the pass-thru shelf. Coffee mugs are stored underneath the counter, out of sight.

Bernice, a woman in her fifties, is discovered seated on stool #7. The stools are numbered 1–7 from stage right to stage left, #4 being the center stool. She is doing "setups," i.e. wrapping sets of silverware — knife, fork, spoon — in individual paper napkins which she then places in a plastic bin. The bin rests on #6. She is seated in profile to us, talking to someone back in the kitchen. (Note: we never see the "people" Bernice talks to or who come into the diner.)

BERNICE. ... so I told 'em, "the hell with it." If it's gonna cost that much to fix the damn thing, I'll just live with it ... What? ... Exactly. Just like your thyroid. You learned to live with that and I'll learn to live with a buzz in my dashboard ... I think it's the radio. They say the speedometer cable, but I say — ... What? ... Naw, I never listen to the damn thing anymore. Nothin' but Jesus and Rush Limbaugh. I used to like that ol' ... what was his name? ... Ernie. Ernie Clapp, when he had that country show out of Emporia. That was good ... That was real good ... But, anymore, you can't tell the difference between country and pop ... and they all do that wiggly stuff with their voices. Hell, just sing the tune, ya know? If I want yodelin' I'll go to Switzerland ... I *wish* ... I wish I could go *some*wheres ... We got a special this mornin', Helen? ... Okay. That's good ... Yeah, I like Italian omelette. So, what happened, you had too much spaghetti sauce left over? ... Well, I told you not to order them big ol' cans. It'd take an army to eat that much I-tie food ... Yeah, I know. I wish we still had the army, too. I told Ezra when they shut down the ordnance depot, I said: "Ezra, your little diner is gonna have a real hard time without them soldier boys comin' in all hours to sober up," and he says: "We'll make it. We been here forever. We'll make it." Well ... 'course it's true, ya know. I mean I can still vaguely remember when they opened this place. His daddy, Irwin, called it the Victory then. The Victory Diner. See, that was after the war ... '48, '49, somethin' like that. I was about five, but I remember Daddy bringin' us all in here — into one of them booths there by the window — *(She points to offstage, right.)* and we got us an ice cream and it was a real big deal. Jesus! Who'd a thunk I'd end up spendin' my entire adult life behind this counter ... Just think o' that, Helen ... *(She has finished, and takes the bin of setups behind the counter, putting them under it, out of sight. She turns on bright neon lights above the passthru.)* I shoulda gone to State. I think I coulda got in. I was pretty good in high school. Nothin' to blow up balloons about, but I did okay. I was *real* good in history. And geography. Isn't that a hoot? Me, who's never been further'n Wichita south or Topeka north ... No, that's not true ... There was that one time I went with ... that guy ... to Santa Fe ... That started out so nice ... *(She exits, left. We hear the refrigerator door open and close. She comes back.)* Helen, we got any G.J. back in the freezer? ... Well, mix me up a pitcher, will ya? We're fresh out and you know ol' crazy Wilma always has to have her grapefruit juice ... "It'll keep me from cancer" ... Where she got that from I'll never know. And her green tea. You ever taste green tea? ... Well, it tastes like somethin' that spent all night in a ditch ... It tastes like water that's been standin' in a Christmas tree holder ... No, I never tasted water that's been standin' in a Christmas tree holder, but it's — ... it's what I *imagine* it to — ... don't bug me, Helen! It's too early in the — *(She looks at her watch.)* Shoot. It's time to open. You all set back there? ... You know Carson'll be here first thing. I got the coffee goin' so I'll go open up. *(She exits, right. We hear her humming as she goes. Pause. She returns.)* That ol' door handle's gonna fall right off. I told Ezra to put in a new one. He never listens. His daddy would never've let the place go to hell like this. He'd never've let him change the name, neither. I liked the "Victory." That big ol' "V" out there with the light bulbs ... Ezra said it looked like a — ... well, never mind what he said it looked like. That man's mind is always in the gutter. But the O-Kay Diner? Just because he married Kaye Kleinfelter and she nagged him into it. Oh yeah, Kaye, that's *real* cute. And o' 'course two years later she ran off to St. Louis. And we're stuck with the O-Kay Diner. So now we got a big ol' "O" with lightbulbs. And I told Ezra what *that* looks like ... *(She suddenly looks stage right where a customer has apparently entered.)* Hi, Carson, how ya be? ... Pull up a plank, honey ... *("Carson" sits at #1.)* I'll get ya some battery acid. *(She gets a mug from beneath the counter and also a setup, which she plunks down at #1. She exits, left, to fill the mug. From off left:)* How's Edna? ... yeah ... *(She returns.)* Oh yeah, I know. That flu is terrible. My Petie had it and he was down for a week. He couldn't go to work. I was afraid they'd fire him ... Over to the lumberyard. You know, Harrison's ... Oh, I know. Petie's scared to death. He says sales are way down. They got so much back inventory stacked up they could rebuild this whole town. Not that anybody'd want to ... Well, you tell Edna to take a lotta C ... Vitamin C ... Oh no, that stuff don't work, Carson, all that herbal shit ... echa-whatever. I took that for a cold and I was sittin' on the can for days; what'll you have today, hon? *(She takes out her order pad and a pencil. Writing:)* ... Uh-huh ... uh-huh ... white or whole wheat? ... No, sometimes you change your mind ... okay, hon. *(To pass-thru.)* Two over easy with pigs and spuds; stack o' dark! ...

    You want some O.J., Carson? ... You still getting' that, whatchamacallit, reflux thing? ... Yeah, it's murder. *(She looks offstage right.)* Hi, Wilma. *(Sotto voce, to "Carson.")* Here comes crazy Wilma. You wanna read a paper or somethin'? ... She'll talk your ear — ... Hi, Wilma! *("Wilma" sits at #6.)* Helen just made up some grapefruit juice for — ... What? ... Oh. Well what *do* you want? ... Prune? Oh yeah, we got prune. Where would this town be without ... *(She exits, left. Returns with a juice glass which she puts down at #6 along with a setup.)* You wanna glass o' water, don't you darlin' ... Oh, Carson I forgot to get you any H2O ... *(She "fills" two glasses and puts them at #1 and #6. Sings:)*

"All day I faced
The barren waste
Without a trace of
Water ... "

(Takes out order pad.) So, Wilma, oatmeal and green tea? ... okay, darlin'. You want raisins in that oatmeal? ... Okay. *(To pass-thru.)* Bowl o' slop; no marbles! I'll get you your tea ... *(Exit left.)*

(From offstage.) What? ... No, Petie's not gettin' married to that girl ... I *wish*. *(She returns. Puts little teapot at #6.)* Why? Honey, I can't get him outta the house. He's not a kid you know ... thirty-seven. He'll be thirty-seven in May ... Otis was thirty-seven when he married you? ... Shoot, I remember that wedding ... You bet your bonnet I was young then. I couldna been more'n — ... *(She goes to pass-thru and picks up plate.)* Here's your feedbag, Carson. *(Puts a ketchup bottle next to his plate.)* I couldna been more'n fifteen, Wilma. And I remember his funeral, too ... Oh, now Wilma, I'm sorry. I didn't mean to ... You've gotta let go, Wilma. It's been near on to twenty years since Otis passed ... Well, it could've happened to anyone, Wilma. *(Beat.)* Anyone who was hangin' from a flagpole ... I know he was upset about that, but ... *(To "Carson.")* The flag got stuck up at the top of that big ol' pole by the post office and Otis wanted it at half-mast 'cause Joe Louis had just died ... I know he did, Wilma. He loved Joe Louis. *(To "Carson.")* Huh? ... '80, '81. Somethin' like that ... oh ... Wilma says it was '81 and she oughta know. Anyway, poor old Otis tried to shinny up that flagpole, but he slipped and — ... All right, Wilma. I'll shut up. I'm sorry, darlin' ... *(Goes to pass-thru.)* ... Here's your oatmeal ... *(Puts bowl at #6.)* See, Carson here is just a youngster; hell, he probably doesn't even know who Joe Louis is ... *was* ... Oh you do? Well good. Anymore you talk to young people — ... Oh you are *so* young, Carson. What are you, twenty-eight? Twenty-nine? ... Oh, big deal: thirty. Carson, that's *young*. I can't even remember thirty. We was livin' over on Monroe when I was thirty. Petie was in grade school. He was ... ten. He had Miss Kromer. *She* was a piece o' work. She told me she thought Petie was

"effeminate." I told her it's too bad she *wasn't*.

My god, Wilma, what are you — ... you're puttin' that prune juice *in* your oatmeal? ... Well, you better hurry on home when you're done, sweetpea. *(Two "strangers" have entered, right.)* Good mornin'. You wanna sit in a booth? ... Sure. Right this way ... *(She exits right. Pause. She returns, goes to pass-thru.)* Helen! Where the hell is Dotty? We got booth customers. That girl is *always* — ... oh, hi Dotty, you come in the back? ... Well, you got two at number 12. *(To offstage right.)* Dotty'll be right with you, folks. *(Sotto voce, to "Carson":)* Dotty looks like death warmed over, what else is new? ... Huh? ... *Yes,* he beats her. He oughta be in jail but she won't tell no one ... Oh no, I'm not gettin' involved. No sir. I'll get you some more joe. *(She heads left. She sees "Carolee" enter, right.)* Hi, Carolee, how are you, sweetheart? *("Carolee" sits at #3.)* What brings you in so early? *(Exits left. Returns with coffeepot and "fills" mug at #1, "Carson." Then, pours one for "Carolee" and places setup.)* Is our friendly mayor still chasin' you around the courthouse? *(To "Wilma.")* Ed Valencin can't keep his horny old hands off Carolee ... O'course Estelle knows. She knows her Ed. He's been chasin' skirts since seventh grade. How's your tea? ... Okay. *(She exits with coffeepot, returns. To "Carolee":)* So. Give me all the gossip. Are we gettin' that juvenile detention center? *(To "Carson.")* Fancy name for reform school. *(To "Carolee.")* No? Shoot. I thought we'd for *sure* get that. No one else wanted the damn thing, and we need it. We got *nothin'*. *(Takes out order pad.)* What do you want, honey? ... That's it?! You can't live on a stack o' toast, Carolee ... You? Why on earth would you be on a diet? A stray breeze and you'll be in Topeka ... All right ... *(To pass-thru.)* A stack o' white, Helen, don't strain yourself ... *(To "Carolee.")* When they closed the high school I knew it was all over for this burg, but then when I heard about the Reform School — the detention deal — I thought, "well, maybe." I mean you need a lotta guards and stuff to give them kids a lickin'. But now that's dead? ... Shoot ... And the Montgomery Ward went out o' business ... What? ... It was? It was two years ago? ... My, time flies when you're dyin' ... *(A "customer" has entered, right. He "sits" at #5.)* Hello there ... And how are you this mornin', sir? ... Well, good. Menu? ... Here ya go ... *(Gives a menu to #5; then goes to pass-thru and gets plate.)* Here's your gourmet breakfast, Carolee. *(To #5.)* What? ... . The special is Italian omelette ... oh it's real

11

good ... *(Takes out order pad.)* ... Uh-huh ... You want hash browns with that? ... okay ... toast? ... oh yeah, we — *(Goes to pass-thru.)* Helen, we got english, don't we? ... Yeah, we got english muffins ... Good. Sounds good ... Hot tea? You got it ... *(She goes to pass-thru.)* Gimme a dago and spuds with english! *(She exits left, returns with tea setup, places it at #5.)* There ya go, sir. You passin' through? ... I see ... Oh, about — Carson, how long's it take to drive to Kansas City? ... Yeah, I thought two and a half, three hours. It's not bad. You go up to Junction City and hang a right on I-70 and then straight through to K.C. ... *(To "Carson.")* Huh? ... He doesn't want to do that! ... *(To #5.)* Oh, he says you could go east on 56 to Council Grove, then over to 335 and north to Topeka, but them are backroads and you don't wanna get lost ... Yeah. Yes, it is. You know about that? ... Well then you *should* go that way. That was the last big stop on the old Santa Fe Trail till they got all the way to Brent Fort out in Colorado ... Oh yeah, I love all that history stuff. We're just three miles north of the Trail here, ya know. I used to — Lost Springs is just three miles south of here and me'n Hawthorne used to go down there and dig ... *(The lights change, darkening subtly and vivid colors seem to reflect off the various glass and silver surfaces.)* ... It was sorta creepy, but it was ... it was good. I mean, you'd find stuff ... old buttons and shotgun shells and stuff ... they went right through there on the Santa Fe Trail. Out o' Missouri — St. Louis and Independence and some big ol' towns that don't exist no more ... Franklin ... and then they'd get to Council Grove on the Neosho River. There's a lake there now, 'cause they damned it up, but back then ... 1840s ... it was just a creek and a lotta hardwood trees: elms and walnut, oak and such. And that would be the end of it. From there on west, it'd be nothin' but prairie and cottonwoods. You can't repair a wagon with cotton-wood, and it don't burn good, neither. So those folks — those husbands and wives and little kids in the wagons and such — they'd kinda look back at Council Grove as they rolled away. They were lookin' back at civilization. For the last time till Santa Fe.

Santa Fe! ... Hawthorne and me, we went down to Santa Fe in '62 ... I was still a kid. Hell, he was takin' a minor across state lines, I guess ... no, maybe not. I was ... Jesus Christ, I was nineteen! Old enough to know better; young enough not to care ... We spent a fabulous weekend there in Santa Fe ... Then Monday mornin' I woke up in that motel and he was gone. I went out in front and the Pontiac was gone. So I figured he went out to get us some breakfast ... that mornin' ... waitin' in that room ... I had to check out at noon. I didn't have but thirty dollars to my name and they took most o' that for the room ... I walked around ol' Santa Fe, sat down in that town square they got ... the plaza there ... Then someone told me about this Traveler's Aid deal, and I went over there and they lent me enough money to hop a bus for Great Bend. Then ol' Myron — my brother — he drove over and got me. He didn't speak to me the whole way home ... and he never really spoke to me since. Well, Myron passed two years ago, so I can't grieve about that ...

He just said one thing to me, he said, "I am so glad momma and poppa are dead. 'Cause this woulda killed 'em." I never did follow the logic of that. But ol' Myron, he was ... strange ...

And I never saw Hawthorne again. But, goddamn, wouldn't you know my Petie looks just like him ... Somedays that makes me happy, and somedays that makes me wanna hit him. I mean, you'd think Hawthorne'd at least — ... What? ... *(Lights restore.)* ... Oh, Carson, you want your check. I'm sorry. I kinda spaced out there, ya know. *(She goes right to the cashier's counter.)* That's, er, ... two-ninety-five and the coffee, and ... three-sixty-seven ... I know, I know: highway robbery. You say that every day and then you come right back and let us rob you again ... *(She mimes taking money and putting it in cashbox. Then, returning, to "Carolee":)* You know Ezra keeps sayin' he's gonna get us — So long, Carson, have a nice day — he's gonna get us a computer cash register. Yeah, that'll be the day. What would we do with a computer? I don't even use that ol' adding machine. I got my own adding machine right here. *(Points to her head. She goes to pass-thru; gives plate to #5.)* Here's that omelet. Doesn't that look yummy? ... Good. *("Ivar" enters and goes to #4.)* Hey, Ivar, how ya be? You just missed Carson ... Whatta you mean? ... Now, Ivar, that was a week ago and it wasn't Carson's fault. You're allowed to turn right on a red light ... We got one traffic light in this town and you pay no attention to it. You just walk right through ... Well, he didn't hit you, did he? He just scared the bejeezus out of you so maybe you'll learn a lesson. You want coffee, hon? ... Okay. *(She exits left for pot, returns.)* You done, Wilma? ... okay, hon ... You leavin' all that money for me? ... Well, bless your heart! ... So long, Wilma. You go straight home now, hear? ... okay

... *(As she takes money to the till, sotto voce:)* That woman is crazy as a loon. She's gonna go out now and rummage through all the trash bins in town lookin' for cans. Then she takes 'em to that place out there on Route 56 where they pay you for 'em. I mean that woman's got more money than God. Otis left her a huge life insurance policy and a pension from the Armstrong plant when it was still workin'. In fact, I sometimes wonder if she didn't grease that ol' flagpole before he started climbin' up ... *(To "Carolee.")* You want some more coffee, Carolee? ... Oh come on. You don't have to run to work. City Hall — which is a joke to begin with; *what* "city"? — City Hall can manage without you for a few more minutes. *(She refills "Carolee's" cup, as, to #5:)* Say what? ... Oh, well now that is a real good question. What *do* we do in this town? See, it used to be real busy. There was the ordnance depot during the war and even up through Vietnam, but that's gone now. And there was the Armstrong plant, they made farm machinery. It's gone. And the farmers around here are all sellin' out. They can't make a dime anymore. Heck, I've had to take in a boarder to make ends meet, and he is strange ... but don't get me off on that. The high school closed last year 'cause there wasn't but seventeen students left in the whole deal. Now they bus the kids over to Council Grove. We still got a post office and a library — and a tavern, of course — but the supermarket's history so we have to drive over to Council Grove or up to Abilene once a week and stock up, or get ripped off at Andy Anderson's little grocery over here on Third — though, you know Carolee, I always try to buy somethin' from him once a week just so *he* won't close. Or there's the 7-11 out on the highway which is a joke. The movie show's been closed for years. There's a pharmacy across from the clinic but if, God forbid, ya gotta go to a real hospital it's twenty miles due east and lots o' luck if you're in labor. Not that anyone around here ever is, cause all the young people move out just as soon as they can. We're the only café in town and can you imagine comin' here for Sunday dinner? ... I know, Helen, I know. You make a lovely pot roast. And your ham steak Hawaiian is to die for. *(She winks at "Carolee.")* ... You made up your mind yet, Ivar? ... It's good; it's Italian omelette ... well, no need to be gross, Ivar. The Italians are wonderful people. Christopher Columbus was Italian — ... What do you mean, he did you no favor? ... Ivar Homlung, you'd be freezin' your butt off in some Norwegian fjord if it weren't for — ... Well then, get mad at Lief Ericson if he got here first. You want a

Norwegian omelet? We'll put some ol' rotten fish and some, whatchamacallem, lingonberries in there and you can scarf *that* down. Honest to God. Now, whatta you want? ... *(Writing on order pad.)* ... okay ... *(Goes to pass-thru.)* Scramble three and ham it up! ... *(To "Ivar.")* What? ... *(To "Helen.")* And a short stack o' cakes. You're gonna get fat, Ivar, eatin' Helen's hotcakes ... Well, then, fatter. *(To #5, pointing at "Ivar.")* Local color. *("Tommy" has entered and goes to #2.)* Oh-oh, here comes the law. Hi, Tommy. *(She puts a setup at #2.)* How we doin' today, hon? ... good ... How's Trudie? *(She gets coffee and gives a mug to "Tommy" as she speaks.)* ... good. She got that skin thing taken care of? ... Oh, I know. It's murder. I get the same thing every winter when I have to wear all that heavy stuff ... Yeah. Whatta you want today, hon, the usual? ... Okie-dokie ... *(To pass-thru.)* Helen, the usual for Tommy ... So, any serial killers out there we oughta know about? This gentleman *(Referring to #5.)* is a tourist so he'll wanna know if it's safe to walk the streets. We haven't had any crime around here since that idiot stole my Petie's Harley — and he didn't get further'n Lost Springs before it fell apart on him. Petie'd been workin' on it the night before and he didn't tighten things up real good, so that guy ended up sittin' in the middle of the highway lookin' like a fool. Was it you brought him in, Tommy? ... Oh. I thought it was you. *(To "Carolee.")* You leavin' hon? ... Well, you have a nice day, now. Let's see ... *(She goes to the cashier's desk.)* You owe me a dollar twenty-five ... 'scuse me, a dollar thirty-one. You gotta stop throwin' your money around, Carolee, you'll end up in the poorhouse. Will we see you at lunch? ... Yogurt?! You're gonna get sick eatin' all that health food. See ya, hon. *(Pause. Then, to "Tommy.")* She's so nice. Why she hangs around this burg I do not know ... Huh? ... Really? I didn't know she was seein' someone. I didn't know there was anyone to see. I tried to talk Petie into takin' her out but ... he wasn't interested. *(She goes to pass-thru; gives plate to "Ivar.")* Here's your grub, Ivar. You want maple syrup? ... Here ya go ... *(Back to "Tommy.")* Did I hear Esther Cravitz passed away last night? ... Did you get called out? ... I heard she dropped dead in her driveway holdin' two sacks of groceries, poor old thing ... Her'n me went to school together. 'Course she was ahead of me. Older, I mean ... No, her Morris passed three years ago ... *(Sotto voce:)* Tommy, did you get a 9-1-1 from Dottie last night? ... Oh, I know, you can't talk about it. But that tells me all I need to know. Why she stays with that big ape I do not know. She's a nice girl ... dumb as a dishrag, but nice ... Well, he oughta be locked up. Oh, I know; it's never her who calls. It's her neighbor, Missy — ... something. She hears all that yellin' and screamin' and she calls you, but Dumb Dottie'll never press charges. "Oh he just had one beer too many." As if that excuses anything. I don't get it. I really don't ... Yeah, ain't love grand, but you still oughta lock him up and eat the key. Does he still work at the gun shop? ... *(To #5.)* That's the only goin' concern in this town. The gun shop. Everybody's armed to the teeth around here. Then in huntin' season they all go out and blow each other's brains out. How many deep-sixed it last huntin' season, Tommy? ... Is that all? Little Stevie Schumacher fell into that ravine ... Yeah, they say he's okay, but he sure blinks a lot. He blinks about a hundred times a minute ... Yeah, he was in here havin' a Coke, poor little guy ... He just sat there ... blinkin' away ... *(She goes to pass-thru.)* Dottie! You got two booths waitin' on you! ... *(She looks at "Tommy" and rolls her eyes. To #5:)* You want more coffee, hon? Oh! You're havin' tea, silly me. You want — ... no? Okay. Tommy, which is the shortest way to K.C.: up through Junction City or over to Council Grove and up that way? This gentleman's goin' up there today ... Well, you explain it to him ...

What's the matter, Ivar? ... What?! ... *(She takes his plate to the pass-thru.)* Helen, Ivar says his eggs are cold ... Don't be vulgar, Helen, just stick 'em in the micro. *("Josie" has entered and sits at #1.)* Hi, Josie! Set right down and make yourself homey ... How are you, hon? ... Oh, I'll be there. Petie'll drive me over. Are those good alleys in Newton? ... Naw. Last time I went bowlin' it was in Salina ... I damn near killed my left knee. You want coffee? ... Yes, ma'am. *(Does coffee and setup.)* What'll you have? ... That's it? A doughnut? ... Suit yourself. If I had to go teach a bunch o' thirdgraders I'd need more'n a — ... Seven? That's all you got? ... You just know they're gonna close that grammar school, Josie ... You teach third *and* fourth? ... Well, that age, they're all the same anyway ... *(She goes to pass-thru.)* Here's your nice *hot* eggs, Ivar ... Yeah, well don't thank *me*. *(To "Josie.")* What kinda doughnut you want, Josie? ... Okay. *(She gets a "doughnut" from the pastry case; serves "Josie.")* Eat it slow, it'll last longer. Them are good doughnuts, Josie. We get 'em delivered fresh. I always take a couple home Saturday nights to have after Sunday mass. My big treat. O' 'course now ... No ... No, I won't do it. I was baptized at St. Joseph's. I went to mass there every Sunday of my life ... That rectory's been sittin' empty for three years, which I think is a *crime*. There are probably homeless folks who could — ... and now we're supposed to drive over to Council Grove to go to mass? ... That's not ... that's not right ... *(Lights subtly change, as before.)* I remember when we had the sisters ... The Sisters of Providence, when we all went to school at St. Joe's ... clear through high school ... I loved ol' Sister Bernadette. She taught seventh grade. Seventh grade is a very important time for a girl, you know. Things are startin' to ... happen. I bust out like a peach tree in July. I was all over myself. Hormone City. Boobs and acne and so self-conscious I couldn't stand to be in the same room with myself. But Sister Bernadette, she understood. She kept me busy so I wouldn't, you know, *dwell* on things. 'Cause, left alone, I'd commence to bawlin' and yellin' for no earthly reason at all. Shoot ... I was a sprawlin' mass of puberty and she kinda gathered me all into a manageable heap. She got me to doin' some real difficult stuff. With my hands, you know. You ever tried smocking? I don't mean with those machine gadgets; I mean by hand. Well, Sister Bernadette — she taught Home Ec to the high school girls — Sister Bernadette and me, we'd sit there after school doin' smocking. We made christening gowns for some of the poor families in town. Now, I was from what could surely be called a poor family, but we didn't talk about that. We talked about the saints. We talked about Saint Bernadette of Lourdes who talked with the Blessed Virgin in that, whatchamacallit, grotto, over in France. I'd dearly love to go there and see that thing. That grotto. I dearly would ...

And the Lady — that's what Sister Bernadette called her — the Lady said: "I am the Immaculate Conception" ... Isn't that beautiful? And people think that means the Virgin Birth, but it don't mean that at all. It means that *she* — her, Mary — was born without original sin. The only one person ever born without — except Jesus, of course, but he wasn't a person. Well, yes he *was* a person but he was also God so, you know, all bets were off.

And we'd talk about those things, up there in the sewing room of the convent. I can smell it: wax. Floor wax and candle wax, 'cause they had this little chapel just two doors down the hall ... And the sisters lived in these little tiny rooms ... one to a room ... all quiet and lovely ... with a holy picture on the wall, and a crucifix ... and a candle ...

I shoulda done that.

I really shoulda.

And now that whole place is gone. The sisters left in the seventies. They'd already gotten rid o' those big ol' habits they used to wear. And then they looked so *dumb* in those grey skirts and blouses; like plucked chicken hens. An' you could tell. They had these forced grins on their faces. And perfect teeth. Nuns have perfect teeth. But you could tell they knew it was all sorta ... dyin' away. And then they just pulled out. Sold the convent to the county. They were gonna use it for a looney bin, but that didn't pan out, so they just tore it down. Put up the Health and Human Services building ... I can't even walk by there — over on Walnut and B. Makes me too sad ... So, I guess it's just as well I didn't become a nun. I only liked it when they wore those big ol' habits with the starched white blinkers and the rosary beads clickin' as they walked ... and those tiny little rooms with the holy pictures ... and the candle ...

And now I don't even go to church anymore. *(Lights slowly restore.)* Why should I, Josie? I mean we are really and truly God-forsaken now, ya know? The Nazarenes still got their church. And they're still jumpin' and speakin' in tongues at the First Assembly, but I don't cotton to any o' that. You know what all that is, Josie? *(Sotto voce.)* S-e-x. They're all gettin' it off to organ music and callin' it the Holy Ghost. Holy Ghost, my hat! Nothin' holy about it. That's called hoopin' and hollerin' where I come from, and there's not a one of them comes outta there with dry underpants ... I'd sooner go to the Methodists and be bored to death ... 'Course, they're gone too ... Everything's gone ... Everything's *gone,* Josie. *(Suddenly strident, harsh.)* Ivar, you eat up those hotcakes, goddamnit! You always do that. You order up a mess o' eggs and spuds and hotcakes and then you leave half of it. No wonder your wife refuses to cook for you ... Aw, shut it, Ivar. Just shut it! You're ugly and you're sloppy and ... you make me *sick,* if you wanna know ... Gimme those dishes. *(She grabs the plate, etc. from his place.)* You get outta here. You go back to poor ol' Mildred and tell her Bernice doesn't want you eatin' here neither!

... Don't tell me what to do, Tommy Hanrahan. Just because you wear a badge and those stupid sunglasses — like you saw on TV or something ... You don't impress me. I remember when you was a little snot-nosed kid. I remember you slashin' tires at the senior prom because what's-her-name, Eulah Munns wouldn't go with you. And you had to do three months of community service, didn't you? —

Don't you butt in, Josie ... *(To #5.)* Listen, mister: You're lucky. You can just drive on through here. Us, we're sentenced to life. You just hop in your car and hit highway 71 or 56 as fast as you can and don't look back, 'cause it'll be like that lady in the Bible if you do. This ol' place is dyin' and you better run before the stench gets to you ...

Why? ... *Why?* I don't know why. Hey, it's the American way, isn't it? The little guys go bust and the Wal-Marts go up and everyone drives thirty miles outta town to save thirty cents ... and the factories move to Mexico or Taiwan or some damn place where they can make little kids work for two bits a day ... And that's the way it is, gang, and here's what we're left with: a literally godforsaken shithole with a greasy spoon café and no schools and four books in the library and nothin' to do nights but watch all the folks on TV havin' fun in the real world miles and miles from here ...

Whatta you mean, I'm just a pessimist! Hell, pessimism looks *good* to me. We're way beyond that. Pessimism left and slammed the screen door years ago.

We're even runnin' outta water. Water's *free.* And we're runnin' out. The Great Aquifer that's underneath this whole part o' the country's bein' pumped dry. I saw that on *60 Minutes*, Josie. You go teach your fourth graders that. Tell 'em to pack their little backpacks and get out *now. (Lights darken.)* ... What are we waitin' for? ... I go home to my thirty-seven-year-old son whose brain has atrophied settin' there lookin' at *Baywatch* reruns and I simply do not know where to turn ... What am I doin' there? ... What am I doin' here? ... The end of the world would be a pleasant alternative to that moment every day when I walk through my front door and step into my parlor and look ... just look ... at ... nothing.

Really nothing.

Nothing at all. *(Pause.)* Sister Bernadette? Sister Bernadette, I am so sorry I didn't listen to you. You said to forget all about ol' Hawthorne and go down to Wichita State and I got so mad at you, I ... I pushed you. I *pushed* you hard. A vessel of the Lord ... *No;* a friend ... And I did that dumb thing and so o' 'course they kicked me out ... What? ... I know ... I know you tried to talk 'em out of it, but I was too all-fired pissed off, and me 'n' Hawthorne went down to Lost Springs and ... and stayed at a ... and that was the

first time we did it. And you know … it wasn't really all that good. You haven't missed a thing, Sister. Oh, it can be good … It was good in Santa Fe. By that time we knew how to do it … I'm sorry. I'm sorry, Sister, I'm embarrassing you. I shouldn't be talkin' about stuff like that … And where are you now? Are you dead? … Are you dead, too? … *(From offstage right, a male Voice.)*
VOICE. Bernice! *(Some bright lights snap on.)*
BERNICE. Aahhh! … Who … who's that?
VOICE. Bernice … what the hell! I have told you over and over again … *(The real Tommy enters. He's a cop in his thirties.)* I have told you. The bank's gonna bring charges against you if they find out. They own this place now. You know that.
BERNICE. *(Timid, like a child.)* I was … I was just gettin' some of my things —
TOMMY. That's what you always say, Bernice.
BERNICE. 'Cause the auction this week, ya know.
TOMMY. Yes, I know. And if there's any of this stuff you want for, you know, old times' sake, well you can come and bid on it then, but you can*not* be comin' in here all hours of the day or night —
BERNICE. I know. I'm sorry, Tommy. I just …
TOMMY. Do you know what time it is, Bernice?
BERNICE. Er … no. I guess it's late, ain't it.
TOMMY. It's three in the morning, Bernice, and I have got better things to do than come in here and —
BERNICE. Three in the morning? They give you the night shift, Tommy? Here, let me get you some coffee.
TOMMY. Bernice, there ain't no coffee! This place has been closed for two and a half months. Ol' Ezra went bust and flew the coop. He's got creditors lookin' for his sorry butt all over Kansas, though if I know Ezra, he's probably up north somewhere. He was always talkin' about Oregon.
BERNICE. Yeah, that's supposed to be real pretty up there.
TOMMY. Uh-huh.
BERNICE. Oregon. *(Pause.)*
TOMMY. Now, Bernice, I want you to put all these things back where they was and I'll drive you home and it'll be our little secret. But this is the last time, okay?
BERNICE. You won't tell Petie?
TOMMY. No, I won't tell Petie. Petie was makin' a fool of himself over at the Pastime last weekend, Bernice. He got all drunked

up and started shoutin' about A-rabs and Moose-lems — that's what he calls 'em, "Moose-lems." And he was out in the street yellin' about A-rabs and sand niggers, and I damn near booked him. But I thought about you, Bernice, and I didn't want to cause you any more grief than you already got. So I just whacked his butt with my nightstick and it scared the shit out of him. Literally. Can't you keep him home nights?
BERNICE. I don't know what he does. I go to bed early.
TOMMY. Yeah. And then you come down here and play make-believe. Honest, Bernice, I oughta send you over to Health and Human Services —
BERNICE. I hate that building.
TOMMY. Building? It ain't even two stories high, Bernice. But they got some people there who could, you know, talk to you.
BERNICE. Sister Bernadette.
TOMMY. Huh?
BERNICE. You wouldn't remember. There used to be a convent there. And then there *was* someone to talk to.
TOMMY. Oh yeah. There used to be nuns. My daddy was taught by them.
BERNICE. Yeah, I knew your daddy.
TOMMY. Sure.
BERNICE. *(Smiling.)* He was a hellion.
TOMMY. You're kiddin' me!
BERNICE. No. Ol' Stevie Hanrahan ... we used to call him Punky.
TOMMY. Why?
BERNICE. I don't know. *(Pause.)*
TOMMY. Bernice?
BERNICE. I know. *(She starts to tidy up, restoring dishes, etc.)*
TOMMY. Nobody wishes this place was still open more'n I do, Bernice. But, anymore, no one's gonna invest in a business here. I sure miss it. I just go to that damn 7-11 and eat my biscuits and gravy in the car. I gotta heat 'em up in a microwave ... I miss the good times we used to have here. But you can't pretend, Bernice. I mean it. They'll send you off to the county hospital with all the loonies. You don't want that.
BERNICE. You won't tell Petie?
TOMMY. *I won't tell Petie!* Jesus ... You got everything?
BERNICE. I guess. *(She is gathering up her purse and coat.)*

TOMMY. Petie still got his job at the lumberyard?
BERNICE. Sort of.
TOMMY. "Sort of" … Jesus. He needs a real kick in the butt, that guy. 'Course then he'd just shit his pants. C'mon, Bernice.
BERNICE. *(Looking around.)* I'm never gonna be here again …
TOMMY. Well, now, you don't know that. I might be wrong about that. Someone might … maybe one of those fast-food deals'll move in here.
BERNICE. I'm not fast enough for fast food.
TOMMY. Oh yes you are. You were the quickest draw on the coffee pot I ever seen.
BERNICE. *(Beaming.)* I was, wasn't I.
TOMMY. Yes you were, Bernice. You were real good.
BERNICE. Yeah.
TOMMY. But it's over now.
BERNICE. Yeah.
TOMMY. All good things … you know.
BERNICE. Uh-huh. *(She doesn't budge.)*
TOMMY. C'mon now, Bernice.
BERNICE. All right, Tommy. Just let me turn off all these neons.
TOMMY. Okay, Bernice. I'll be out front.
BERNICE. Right. Thanks, Tommy.
TOMMY. Uh-huh. Don't linger, now … *(He looks at her for a moment, then exits, right. Bernice notices a juice glass on the counter — "Wilma's" — and she puts it away. She goes to the pass-thru.)*
BERNICE. So long, Helen. I, er … I won't be in tomorrow. You take care o' yourself, now. I worry about you, ya know, I — … and don't order any — … I mean … (She turns out the neon lights.) You take care o' yourself … *(Bernice exits, right. Pause. Other lights snap off. We hear a door close off right. The diner is left in near darkness, only a nightlight glowing somewhere, then it, too, fades to black.)*

End of Part One

PART TWO

THE BUTTERFLY EFFECT

In the darkness, a voice is heard:

VOICE. ... and now it is my privilege and pleasure to introduce this year's Grand Laureate of the American Philosophical Society, who will deliver the annual Alfred G. Hesseltine Lecture. *(Applause heard, dying out as lights come up to reveal: Randall, at a speaker's lectern. To his right, a blackboard on an easel. The stage is oddly bare, but for a hanging object upstage, a shrouded picture frame. There is a door upstage left, closed. Mid-stage right is a low cabinet. Randall is fortyish, wears reading glasses which he takes on and off as the mood hits him. He is unremarkable, but is wearing an academic robe. He is clean-shaven and wears his hair in a slightly eccentric manner; it is, perhaps, a shade too long. Perhaps it has been colored to appear younger, but nothing blatant or farcical. He occasionally reads from notes.)*

RANDALL. Mr. Chairman, former laureates, distinguished colleagues, and friends. It is indeed humbling to find oneself here ... and one may consequently ask: Is that the nature of self-perception? Do we "find" ourselves, i.e., is self-cognition a series of accidental revelations, and if so, who is the revealer? ... which could, of course, lead to phenomenological — if, not to say, theological speculations of the worst kind ... but I digress.

It is indeed humbling to stand before this distinguished body ... if all of you in your particularities can be categorized not as particulates but as a whole ... "whole" with a "w" ...

It is indeed humbling to attain cognition of the fact that I *am* ... well, we won't get into that ... that I have been *named* Grand Laureate of the year by this demanding assembly.

And I thank you.

Humbly.

If humility is even a possibility, for in the saying of it, e.g.: "In my humble opinion" we mean, of course, the exact opposite. Is it possible, even, to profess humility without at the same time patting oneself on the self-referential back for having attained to that virtue, ergo canceling out the condition? It would be truer, would it not, to say: "I am proud as punch to be named laureate, and about time, too!"

I jest.

And I digress.

It has been customary for the Alfred G. Hesseltine Lecturer to deal with an explication of his — or conceivably her — main body of published text. But I demur. I shall, instead, discuss — as much for my own illumination as for yours — the problem of my current work in progress, *De Defictionis Natura; The Nature of Failure*.

As ninety percent of humankind considers itself to have failed, and ninety-five percent actually have ... oh, perhaps I am being ungenerous; ninety-seven percent actually have, is nearer the mark ... it is good to explore the nature and positive values of failure. We all know — too well — or think we know that we know the negative aspects. For once one perceives oneself ... "finds oneself"? ... a success, life ends.

Life. Ends. Life in the Hegelian, Marxist construct; life as dialectic struggle.

Is, then, failure even possible? Or is it merely the sum of our retrenchments? Spring forward. Fall back. To spring again.

Is failure simply the inevitable wintering of our diurnal progress?

(And we will not discuss the nature of Progress.)

But if, for every thesis there is an antithesis, and never a synthesis, is not that, then, a failed progression? Winter kill. No spring. April Fool.

I want.

I can't get.

End of process.

Back to primal zero.

Can't go home again.

Go instead to bottle or refrigerator, or shopping mall, or to the violence of sex ...

Wildflowers ...

Excuse me; I digress.

Or, to put it in terms we all can understand: *(He goes to the black-*

board. Writing:) x = thesis

-y = antithesis

For, anything antithetical is necessarily a negative value. Ergo: *(Writing:)* x + (-y) ... which is ... x — y = X1

And so forth: *(Writing:)* x1 ... n + (-y1 ... n.) = Xn

But, you see, what actually occurs in life is that "y" has a greater value — albeit negative — than "x" in almost every case. So that, *(Writing.)* x + (-y) = x - y = - y ... and x disappears. E.g.:

Our brave new, wished-for X1 is negative, is in fact simply negated by "y," the triumph of antithesis.

So, the vice-president of the corporation — we'll call him "x" — wanting to become the president, X1, must confront: *(Drawing:)* ... the politically correct sales manager, "y," who has married the president's daughter with the alarming bosom and irritating habit of saying "okey-dokey!" And our vice-president who has nothing but skill and experience going for him is simply overwhelmed; negated. Not only does he remain a small "x," but he is fired by the sales manager — now president ... *(Writes:)* Y1

The Super-Y.

"x" is now a negative x1. He is less than zero. He has ...

(He draws a line through x.)

... *failed.*

And Super-Y? He now wishes to become Chairman of the Board. But so does the chairman's son, a repulsive young man interested only in stock car racing and the transmitting of various social diseases. But nepotism has strong numerical value, let me tell you. And so on and so on and so on.

If one were to graph x's life, all we would really see is a descending curve if not a total collapse. For most of us it is a horizontal line. Nary a hillock nor bump discernable. A line one cannot even see. A point.

But there is something missing here. We are describing life as linear. Life is *not (He puts his right hand into a pocket.)* linear! *(Sound: applause heard.)* Now, some of you will cry "Foul" because my analysis is teleological, positing some sort of end or target or design. They will demand facticity, merely. Perhaps I suffer from intrinsic deference to Schopenhauer's Universal Will, to that strong Germanic north wind pushing us ever onward, or rebuffing us ever backward ... But the Individual may rebel, may demur, may deny. "Where there's a will there's a Nay"? *(Hand in pocket again. Sound:*

applause.) Thank you.

Yet even without Will or an Absolute ... pace, Heidegger ... who was a Jesuit and *then* a Nazi ... to which I reply, "of *course*" ... but I digress.

I ... *(He looks through his notes. He is lost.)* ... Levi-Strauss! ... .No, that's not it ... linear ... *function!* Yes!

These ruminations and equations are linear, but life is merely a Function *(Writes: F.)* of constantly variable ... variables. *(Writes: $X1 = F\, dx/dy$.)* We are dealing with differentials and as we all know differential equations are rarely solvable. So, zeitgeist or no zeitgeist, what is the factor which constantly alters our progress? It is a pure accidental. It is the grain of sand in the pendulum. It is ...

Can the flapping of a butterfly's wing in Ulan Bator, Mongolia in May of 2000 eventually cause tropical storm Angelina in the Azores in 2001?

Theoretically, yes. But also *practically* yes. Yes, you bet your booty, yes!

The famous butterfly. The basis of Chaos Theory — or one of them, for chaos is too random to admit to a basis. The Butterfly Effect ... *(Pause. Hand in pocket. Applause. The applause won't stop. He yanks the remote control device from his pocket, aiming it at the cabinet, stage right. Applause keeps on. Finally, he goes to the cabinet, opens it to reveal a tape deck, amp, etc. He angrily turns off the power and then skulks back to the lectern.)*

But I digress.

No, I don't. *(Pause.)* Little Mary wishes — for reasons known only to herself — to be a podiatrist. Accordingly she studies and makes great strides — tee-hee — to get, as it were, a leg up, or perhaps more appropriately, a firm footing in things podiatric by following a course of pre-med studies at the state university. One day she *spills coffee* on her blouse during breakfast and goes back to her room to change. In the hall she meets her friend ... Ashley, who is weeping having just learned of her father's sudden demise, the result of his missing a rung on a ladder while cleaning a leaf-clogged gutter. Mary drops everything, as it were, and accompanies the grieving Ashley to her room. She misses, therefore, the anatomy seminar on the optic nerve and retro bulbar neuritis, chaired by visiting physician, Dr. Felix Mainwright, whose specialty it is.

Two years later, at her oral exam, a vital question arises concerning the optic nerve, about which Mary's knowledge is hazy bordering on non-existent. And the guest examiner is someone she has never seen before, who inquires, "Weren't you at my seminar two Aprils ago?" And Mary remembers the weeping Ashley, the accident-prone father, and tries wildly to explain all that to the unsympathetic F. Mainwright, optical neurologist extraordinaire who has no patience with those who lose their footing.

And Mary fails. And she becomes, instead, a real estate agent in a depressed community, turns to calories for comfort and is eventually dismissed by the real estate agency because her obesity and consequent torpor are antithetical to the agency's motto: "Get up and go; let up and you're gone."

Mary, failed podiatrist and realtor, wallows in her failure and sinks into the Slough of Despond. She blames it on *Ashley*. She blames it on Ashley's maladroit sire. She has forgotten: *the coffee stain*. The tiny accidental that caused it all. Or, perhaps, that leaf which was the last leaf to clog the gutter which Ashley, père, sought vainly, fatally to dislodge.

"How bizarre," I hear you say. But I will ask you to know your communal self. Examine origins. You were conceived, yes, on some emotional occasion — it is devoutly to be wished — by two persons of opposing genders who found themselves in connubial bliss ... or at least lubricious engagement ... but how did that occur? Because they met one another, perhaps at a social event, perhaps on a tour bus or perhaps in the imported carpet department of some large Midwestern emporium. But what brought them there? And what coincided to cause *their* progenitors to make the beast with two backs, and how did *they* meet, and was it because an elevator stalled or a streetcar arrived at precisely 4:17 P.M. that rainy Thursday in Toledo ... etc., etc., etc. One could run mad tracing back to origins. To the Prime Mover, if one were of the Deistic persuasion. Between that first Big Bang and all the subsequent whimpers, there is nothing but an ... endless? ... perhaps ... series of accidents, a cacophony of butterfly wings fanning us down to dismay ...

And our wished-for progress will forever be subjected to this infinitesimal and constantly variable ... *(He draws on board: R.)* "R" ... for random ... whose value is ... indeterminate.

So that all this ... *(Pointing to equations, etc.)* ... is meaningless.

Because failure is meaningless. *(He writes: Q.E.D. Pause.)*

Principia Mathematica be damned. *(He violently erases the blackboard.)* Meaning. Less. *(Pause.)* When I matriculated ... filthy sounding word and, come to think of it, it *is* often self-abuse ... I matriculated at the University of Iowa. A mistake. Oh, nothing wrong with Iowa. Lovely town, Iowa City. Lots of green. And water. But I was hungry. Coming from the hick-town hellhole of my youth, the total disdain of my ... progenitors ... taking my revenge through Language, I talked them to death. They couldn't understand, my poor, dusty parents, one word I said and I *loved* it. I gloated.

Well.

They're both dead.

Ha ha.

Farm machinery. Rude mechanicals.

I wanted to know *everything*. Studied philosophy, history, mathematics, literature ... *Latin.* Yes. I and two gray girls. Twenty years old, already gray. Oh, not their hair, no, their ... aura. Switched to Italian hoping the girls would be less gray ... like Nancy Puglesi ... who was kind to me. Once.

I digress.

Couldn't focus on any one thing; I was frantic. I majored in the History of Ideas and received a completely useless degree.

And then St. Edward's.

Upscale. Prep school. Rich Catholic boys. Taught them history. And Latin. They called me — ... never mind.

I took a group of them ...

Listen to me now; this is the Randall K. Kleinfelter Lecture on Failure. It's a required course, folks. Take notes. There will be a quiz.

Which you will *fail!*

F.

The F-word. The real one. *(Pause.)* I took my history class to see the Mormon Trail. To see where those industrious, God-fearing, enterprising loonies cried "Westward Ho" and dragged their several wives across the prairies to populate Utah with their exorbitant fry.

Late May and already humid, we came to the river ...

Christopher. No. That was earlier ... *(Lights begin to dim somewhat.)* Christopher, when I was twelve.

Christopher and I bicycled out to Sanderson Pond to get

away from the heat. Took off our shoes and went wading, and then — when we saw how alone we truly were — we ... he dared me and I double-dared him and we took off our clothes and fell into the cool waters of Sanderson Pond.

I do not digress.

Then we lay in the prairie grasses.

Wildflowers.

And we were, too. So young and blooming then. Looked straight up at the afternoon, hot-blue sky. *(Pause.)* When a butterfly came and settled on my — ... thing ... my ... sex ... my ... PENIS! Let's call a spade a spade!

Well, my hormones, young and pumping, had been on battle-alert for months, and I ... erected.

Straight as a flagpole. A wondrous thing to behold at the base of one's flat twelve-year-old belly. And Christopher laughed. And then the same thing happened to Christopher. Not the butterfly, no. The butterfly, the prime mover, had fluttered away in lepidotric amazement.

So we lay there ... no, sat there now, gazing in wonder at these cylindrical manifestations. And then ... impulsively ... I touched him. There. And he erupted.

We had never seen that phenomenon before.

And we were sore afraid.

Christopher, shamed and startled ... and scared ... cleansing himself with grasses and wildflowers ... clumsily pulling on shorts, jeans, his ... green plaid shirt ... runs to his bicycle. I struggle to follow, tripping over my trousers, fumbling with shoes and socks ... "Christopher!" ... Gone.

I bicycle slowly home. Alone and as filled with shame as the old, biblical men who gazed upon Susannah where she bathed ...

I who had done nothing wrong.

We never spoke again.

And I was turned out of the Garden of Eden. *(Pause. Lights restore.)* So, then, years later, by the waters of the Iowa my history class and I ... late May and already humid ... "Let's go in!" cries one. "Last one in is a Communist," cries another. And before I can protest, before I can say: "I cannot be responsible ... for *anything*," they are naked and splashing like wild young colts at the watering hole, splendidly raw after a lifetime of Catholic reserve.

After a time, one of them ... Dealy ... we always called

them by last names as if we were at Eton ... Dealy came up onto the bank complaining of leeches or tadpoles and I laughed. He brushed himself off and stood there, golden in the sun, and said to me: "This is beautiful." Which it was. And I, thrilled that he could say that — such things are hard to say at that cynical age — thrilled that he could see the beauty of the moment and of his proud youth ... I ... impulsively ... *Why* did I?! ... reached out and touched him. Oh no, not *there*. Heavens no. Touched him ... I'm not sure where. Later he would say, "On my flank." Where the hell is a flank?

I don't know. On his side. On his hip. I don't remember, but not *there*.

It was a damn silly thing. I didn't think about it. It occurred.

Random.

The second landing of the butterfly.

He didn't say a word. Turned beet-red and went to his clothing. Not a word was said about it to the others and we made our way back to St. Edward's in the smelly van.

Three days later. Summoned to the headmaster.

One week later I was gone. Dismissed.

The parents did not press charges. *(Pause.)* I thought, perhaps in another state. I thought, perhaps in Kansas, for heaven's sake. But no. "One must supply references." *(Pause.)* Ha ha.

No kindness could I expect from St. Edward. Edward the Confessor.

And I have never touched anyone since. Nor shall I. *(He walks aimlessly around the room. Impulsively, he darts to the cabinet, pushes a button. Applause is heard. He turns it off. He leans on the lectern.)* I have never been to New York.

I have never been to Chicago. *(Beat.)* I've been to Des Moines.

I was very nervous there. I have difficulty with people. *(Pause.)* I have never been to New York or Chicago or San Francisco ... or Boston ... or Rio de Janeiro. Or Paris. And I never will.

I'd never get on an airplane. Wouldn't dare. I have to be in complete control, you see, because *one* slip, one unattended moment, and ...

Mr. Chairman, former laureates, distinguished colleagues and friends: You have never accepted me into the American Philosophical Society despite my *repeated* requests — both by mail and by telephone — falling back on the tedious excuse that a higher academic standing and publications were minimal requirements. Minimal for *you*, maybe ...

I have much to tell you.

To reiterate: The Nature of Failure.

De Defictionis — *(There is a knock at the door upstage left.)*
FEMALE VOICE. Professor?
RANDALL. I am not a professor! *Why* do you — ... *(He goes to door and opens it, revealing Bernice.)* Why do you insist on calling me "professor"? Do I *look* like a — *(He realizes he is wearing academic robes.)* Oh.
BERNICE. I thought you liked bein' called Professor, Randy.
RANDALL. Ran*dall*. My name is Ran*dall*. Randy is a condition of goats and old lechers.
BERNICE. Huh?
RANDALL. What do you want?
BERNICE. You had a phone message.
RANDALL. I?
BERNICE. Andy wants you down to the grocery. Loretta's home sick and he's got a bunch of stock to shelf so he wants you down there A.S.A.P. to work the checkout.
RANDALL. This is my morning off. I do afternoons on Thursday.
BERNICE. Well, Loretta's sick.
RANDALL. Loretta is always sick. "Female" troubles. What is it with you? I think you were badly designed. If you were cars you'd be recalled.
BERNICE. He says get there at least by ten. You want me to make you some breakfast, hon?
RANDALL. No, no ...
BERNICE. You can't live on air, ya know.
RANDALL. I know ... I ...
BERNICE. *(Seeing the lectern.)* What the hell is that?
RANDALL. That is a lectern, Bernice. I purchased it from an ecclesiastical supply firm in Wichita. By mail.
BERNICE. I wondered what that big ol' package was.
RANDALL. I assembled it myself. I use it to practice. So that when I return to my chosen — ...
BERNICE. Well, it looks real nice, Rand — ... all. See, that's why I call you Professor, 'cause, you know, you used to —
RANDALL. Sham! *(Pause.)* All a sham. I couldn't teach anyone

anything. Do you think I'd be here in this hellhole hick town, living in a rented room? Working as a grocery clerk? Feeling my brain … mind … atrophy? I who have read Kant, Hegel, Kierkegaard … Heidegger. Not to mention Cicero, Virgil … dear, beloved Juvenal … for what? For *what?*

No.

That's not it.

I have suffered from the delusion that progress is a possibility. And yet one false step. One impulsive — … And I don't know why I did it. I meant no harm, Bernice, no harm at all. I know you believe me, Bernice. You're a good woman. Would I harm a child? A young … god … golden in the sun … O wonderful to behold …

No.

That's not it.

I'm terrified, you see. It's better for me to be here. A room in someone else's house. No responsibilities. A tiny, piece-of-shit, excuse me Bernice, town with no one who comes near or even comes *close* to me in learning.

Slipping away now …

For instance, I used to have a smattering of literary Italian. I used to read Dante … sort of. Now all I remember are operatic phrases and what good are they?

"E avanti a lui tremava tutta Roma."

Well.
BERNICE. That's pretty. *(Pause.)*
RANDALL. I'm afraid to go to Kansas City. If someone were to speak rudely to me, I'd want to tell them: "You! What do you know about me? I who have read Sartre." And Sartre was right, Bernice. Don't give a damn. Live by your own rules.

No.

That's not it. *(Pause.)* I go about in a half-life. Wearing false robes. *(He tears off his academic robe. He is in a tee shirt and boxer shorts.)* There! *Ecce Homo*; behold the man. *(Pause.)*
BERNICE. Andy wants you there at ten. *(He slumps to his knees.)*
RANDALL. Aahhhh! Yes. *Yes.* That's it! There's the bitter truth. There's the meaning of it. The meaning of the meaning: Andy wants me at ten o'clock. On these words shall I build my life!
BERNICE. *(Sternly.)* Hey! Be happy you *got* a job, mister. Some of us — …

RANDALL. Oh yes. I'm happy! *(He leaps to his feet.)* I'm delirious. I leap to bliss like an African springbok! *O goia! Ach Gluck!* I shall go now to Innisfree! *(He runs off right. Great clattering noises of bureau drawers being opened and slammed shut, closet doors, etc. Bernice picks up his academic robe and hangs it carefully over the lectern. She goes to the cabinet, right, and looks at the tape deck. She pushes what she thinks is the power button. Instead, loud applause comes over speakers.)*

BERNICE. AAHHHhhh! *(Randall reenters dressed in trousers and a white uniform shirt that says "Anderson's Grocery" on the back and on the front shirt pocket. He sports a clip-on bow tie. The applause is still on. He bows profusely.)*

RANDALL. Thank you ... *thank* you ... Ah, you really shouldn't ... Please! I am unworthy ... I am — *(Bernice succeeds in shutting off the tape. Pause.)* I shall probably live here for the rest of my life, Bernice. What do you say to that?

BERNICE. Well ... you might wanna get a TV.

RANDALL. What would I possibly watch on a television set?

BERNICE. Well, there's ballgames, you know, and —

RANDALL. Bernice, how can you stand the idea of my being here forever? Like the mad woman in the attic? In *Jane Eyre*.

BERNICE. Jane...?

RANDALL. I won't hurt you, Bernice. I would never hurt you.

BERNICE. You better not, 'cause I'll beat the crap outta you.

RANDALL. Yes! That's good. We have an understanding then.

BERNICE. Fine.

RANDALL. *(Hesitantly.)* And if ... when it snows ... you need some help. You know.

BERNICE. Help?

RANDALL. Shoveling.

BERNICE. Oh. *(Beat.)* Sure.

RANDALL. Splendid. Fine. We have a relationship. *(He starts to leave; turns back.)* Of course, it may not snow.

BERNICE. *(Nods, to humor him.)* Er ... uh-huh.

RANDALL. Random. The R factor. It depends on what's happening in Ulan Bator. *(Beat.)*

BERNICE. Andy wants you there at ten.

RANDALL. Yes!

That's it.

I must go now. I am "expected." What a wonderful thing to

be … expected! *(He exits, door upstage left. Bernice is left, bewildered. She walks towards the door. Stops. Looks back at the covered picture which has been hanging there all this time. She checks to see that Randall has truly gone. She gingerly pulls the cloth away from the picture, revealing an ornate gilt frame displaying a collection of brightly colored, splendidly mounted butterflies. Lights fade to black.)*

End of Play

PROPERTY LIST

Coffee cups, coffee pot
Silverware rolled in napkins
Plates, bowls, water glasses
Menus
Diner accoutrements
Ketchup bottle, syrup bottle
Teapot
Purse and coat
Lectern
Remote control
Notes
Tape deck
Chalkboard, chalk

SOUND EFFECTS

Applause

NEW PLAYS

★ **THE GREAT AMERICAN TRAILER PARK MUSICAL music and lyrics by David Nehls, book by Betsy Kelso.** Pippi, a stripper on the run, has just moved into Armadillo Acres, wreaking havoc among the tenants of Florida's most exclusive trailer park. "Adultery, strippers, murderous ex-boyfriends, Costco and the Ice Capades. Undeniable fun." –*NY Post*. "Joyful and unashamedly vulgar." –*The New Yorker*. "Sparkles with treasure." –*New York Sun*. [2M, 5W] ISBN: 978-0-8222-2137-1

★ **MATCH by Stephen Belber.** When a young Seattle couple meet a prominent New York choreographer, they are led on a fraught journey that will change their lives forever. "Uproariously funny, deeply moving, enthralling theatre." –*NY Daily News*. "Prolific laughs and ear-to-ear smiles." –*NY Magazine*. [2M, 1W] ISBN: 978-0-8222-2020-6

★ **MR. MARMALADE by Noah Haidle.** Four-year-old Lucy's imaginary friend, Mr. Marmalade, doesn't have much time for her—not to mention he has a cocaine addiction and a penchant for pornography. "Alternately hilarious and heartbreaking." –*The New Yorker*. "A mature and accomplished play." –*LA Times*. "Scathingly observant comedy." –*Miami Herald*. [4M, 2W] ISBN: 978-0-8222-2142-5

★ **MOONLIGHT AND MAGNOLIAS by Ron Hutchinson.** Three men cloister themselves as they work tirelessly to reshape a screenplay that's just not working—*Gone with the Wind*. "Consumers of vintage Hollywood insider stories will eat up Hutchinson's diverting conjecture." –*Variety*. "A lot of fun." –*NY Post*. "A Hollywood dream-factory farce." –*Chicago Sun-Times*. [3M, 1W] ISBN: 978-0-8222-2084-8

★ **THE LEARNED LADIES OF PARK AVENUE by David Grimm, translated and freely adapted from Molière's *Les Femmes Savantes*.** Dicky wants to marry Betty, but her mother's plan is for Betty to wed a most pompous man. "A brave, brainy and barmy revision." –*Hartford Courant*. "A rare but welcome bird in contemporary theatre." –*New Haven Register*. "Roll over Cole Porter." –*Boston Globe*. [5M, 5W] ISBN: 978-0-8222-2135-7

★ **REGRETS ONLY by Paul Rudnick.** A sparkling comedy of Manhattan manners that explores the latest topics in marriage, friendships and squandered riches. "One of the funniest quip-meisters on the planet." –*NY Times*. "Precious moments of hilarity. Devastatingly accurate political and social satire." –*BackStage*. "Great fun." –*CurtainUp*. [3M, 3W] ISBN: 978-0-8222-2223-1

DRAMATISTS PLAY SERVICE, INC.
440 Park Avenue South, New York, NY 10016 212-683-8960 Fax 212-213-1539
postmaster@dramatists.com   www.dramatists.com

NEW PLAYS

★ **AFTER ASHLEY by Gina Gionfriddo.** A teenager is unwillingly thrust into the national spotlight when a family tragedy becomes talk-show fodder. "A work that virtually any audience would find accessible." –*NY Times.* "Deft characterization and caustic humor." –*NY Sun.* "A smart satirical drama." –*Variety.* [4M, 2W] ISBN: 978-0-8222-2099-2

★ **THE RUBY SUNRISE by Rinne Groff.** Twenty-five years after Ruby struggles to realize her dream of inventing the first television, her daughter faces similar battles of faith as she works to get Ruby's story told on network TV. "Measured and intelligent, optimistic yet clear-eyed." –*NY Magazine.* "Maintains an exciting sense of ingenuity." –*Village Voice.* "Sinuous theatrical flair." –*Broadway.com.* [3M, 4W] ISBN: 978-0-8222-2140-1

★ **MY NAME IS RACHEL CORRIE taken from the writings of Rachel Corrie, edited by Alan Rickman and Katharine Viner.** This solo piece tells the story of Rachel Corrie who was killed in Gaza by an Israeli bulldozer set to demolish a Palestinian home. "Heartbreaking urgency. An invigoratingly detailed portrait of a passionate idealist." –*NY Times.* "Deeply authentically human." –*USA Today.* "A stunning dramatization." –*CurtainUp.* [1W] ISBN: 978-0-8222-2222-4

★ **ALMOST, MAINE by John Cariani.** This charming midwinter night's dream of a play turns romantic clichés on their ear as it chronicles the painfully hilarious amorous adventures (and misadventures) of residents of a remote northern town that doesn't quite exist. "A whimsical approach to the joys and perils of romance." –*NY Times.* "Sweet, poignant and witty." –*NY Daily News.* "Aims for the heart by way of the funny bone." –*Star-Ledger.* [2M, 2W] ISBN: 978-0-8222-2156-2

★ **Mitch Albom's TUESDAYS WITH MORRIE by Jeffrey Hatcher and Mitch Albom, based on the book by Mitch Albom.** The true story of Brandeis University professor Morrie Schwartz and his relationship with his student Mitch Albom. "A touching, life-affirming, deeply emotional drama." –*NY Daily News.* "You'll laugh. You'll cry." –*Variety.* "Moving and powerful." –*NY Post.* [2M] ISBN: 978-0-8222-2188-3

★ **DOG SEES GOD: CONFESSIONS OF A TEENAGE BLOCKHEAD by Bert V. Royal.** An abused pianist and a pyromaniac ex-girlfriend contribute to the teen-angst of America's most hapless kid. "A welcome antidote to the notion that the *Peanuts* gang provides merely American cuteness." –*NY Times.* "Hysterically funny." –*NY Post.* "The *Peanuts* kids have finally come out of their shells." –*Time Out.* [4M, 4W] ISBN: 978-0-8222-2152-4

DRAMATISTS PLAY SERVICE, INC.
440 Park Avenue South, New York, NY 10016 212-683-8960 Fax 212-213-1539
postmaster@dramatists.com   www.dramatists.com

NEW PLAYS

★ **RABBIT HOLE by David Lindsay-Abaire.** Winner of the 2007 Pulitzer Prize. Becca and Howie Corbett have everything a couple could want until a life-shattering accident turns their world upside down. "An intensely emotional examination of grief, laced with wit." –*Variety.* "A transcendent and deeply affecting new play." –*Entertainment Weekly.* "Painstakingly beautiful." –*BackStage.* [2M, 3W] ISBN: 978-0-8222-2154-8

★ **DOUBT, A Parable by John Patrick Shanley.** Winner of the 2005 Pulitzer Prize and Tony Award. Sister Aloysius, a Bronx school principal, takes matters into her own hands when she suspects the young Father Flynn of improper relations with one of the male students. "All the elements come invigoratingly together like clockwork." –*Variety.* "Passionate, exquisite, important, engrossing." –*NY Newsday.* [1M, 3W] ISBN: 978-0-8222-2219-4

★ **THE PILLOWMAN by Martin McDonagh.** In an unnamed totalitarian state, an author of horrific children's stories discovers that someone has been making his stories come true. "A blindingly bright black comedy." –*NY Times.* "McDonagh's least forgiving, bravest play." –*Variety.* "Thoroughly startling and genuinely intimidating." –*Chicago Tribune.* [4M, 5 bit parts (2M, 1W, 1 boy, 1 girl)] ISBN: 978-0-8222-2100-5

★ **GREY GARDENS book by Doug Wright, music by Scott Frankel, lyrics by Michael Korie.** The hilarious and heartbreaking story of Big Edie and Little Edie Bouvier Beale, the eccentric aunt and cousin of Jacqueline Kennedy Onassis, once bright names on the social register who became East Hampton's most notorious recluses. "An experience no passionate theatergoer should miss." –*NY Times.* "A unique and unmissable musical." –*Rolling Stone.* [4M, 3W, 2 girls] ISBN: 978-0-8222-2181-4

★ **THE LITTLE DOG LAUGHED by Douglas Carter Beane.** Mitchell Green could make it big as the hot new leading man in Hollywood if Diane, his agent, could just keep him in the closet. "Devastatingly funny." –*NY Times.* "An out-and-out delight." –*NY Daily News.* "Full of wit and wisdom." –*NY Post.* [2M, 2W] ISBN: 978-0-8222-2226-2

★ **SHINING CITY by Conor McPherson.** A guilt-ridden man reaches out to a therapist after seeing the ghost of his recently deceased wife. "Haunting, inspired and glorious." –*NY Times.* "Simply breathtaking and astonishing." –*Time Out.* "A thoughtful, artful, absorbing new drama." –*Star-Ledger.* [3M, 1W] ISBN: 978-0-8222-2187-6

DRAMATISTS PLAY SERVICE, INC.
440 Park Avenue South, New York, NY 10016 212-683-8960 Fax 212-213-1539
postmaster@dramatists.com www.dramatists.com